Managing Editor
Karen J. Goldfluss, M.S. Ed.

Editor-in-Chief
Sharon Coan, M.S. Ed.

Illustrators
Howard Chaney
Bruce Hedges

Cover Artist
Lesley Palmer

Art Coordinator
Kevin Barnes

Art Director
CJae Froshay

Imaging
Rosa C. See

Product Manager
Phil Garcia

Publisher
Mary D. Smith, M.S. Ed.

W9-DGK-796

The Human Body

SUPER SCIENCE ACTIVITIES

Written by Ruth M. Young, M.S. Ed.

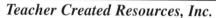

Teacher Created Resources, Inc.
6421 Industry Way
Westminster, CA 92683
www.teachercreated.com

ISBN: 978-0-7439-3662-0

©*2002 Teacher Created Resources, Inc.*
Reprinted, 2009
Made in the U. S. A.

Teacher Created Resources

Table of Contents

Introduction

Students begin a study of the body with a look at their teeth. The children check to see what teeth they presently have. They will learn how the eye adjusts to bright and dim light, as well as discover the parts of the eye. The brain is investigated through a variety of activities, including testing reflexes, relaying a message, and relearning how to write their names. Muscles will be investigated by examining a chicken thigh and leg, as well as watching what happens when the muscles in their own faces are used to make expressions.

The study of the skeleton leads students inside the body. Bones found in owl pellets are used to help students see the shapes and placement of bones. These are compared to their own. Breathing is investigated through the construction of a lung model and blowing bubbles. The study moves on to the heart where students learn how blood circulates through the body by following a blood cell through this important muscle.

Children are always curious about what happens to the food they eat. The activities on walking through the digestive system and simulating the trip of a banana through the intestine will help them understand this process.

Next, students participate in activities that lay the foundation for good nutrition. They review the nutritional value of a variety of foods, examine their personal eating habits, and learn about the foods that contribute to a healthy diet.

As a culminating activity for this study, students will place the internal organs and bones inside a body outline.

A Look at My Teeth

Teacher Information

Look at the drawings and information about primary and permanent teeth on page 5, provided for the teacher as background. It is not important that students learn the terminology or predicted age of emergence of the teeth.

Overview: *Students will learn about their teeth and make a record of their present teeth.*

Materials

- x-rays of teeth (Ask your dentist for these.)
- examples of actual teeth
- mirrors (one per student)
- toothpicks
- Here Are My Teeth activity sheet (page 5)
- transparency of Inside a Tooth (page 6)

Lesson Preparation

- Ask your dentist for x-rays of teeth from children and adults.
- Also request teeth specimens, molds, and photographs, as well as booklets on growth and care of the teeth.

Activity

1. Ask students to feel their teeth with their tongues to see if all of them are exactly alike. Discuss the differences. Ask them if they have any missing teeth. If so, let them feel with their tongues to see if they can feel the new tooth pushing up through the gum. Discuss what it feels like to lose a tooth. Tell them that this is a natural part of growing up.

2. Give each student a mirror and the activity sheet. Show the transparency of this sheet and use it to show students how to place an X on primary teeth which are missing. Explain that they should use the toothpick along with the mirror to locate their teeth, counting from the center front to know where these are on the chart.

3. Let students begin to examine their teeth and record those which are missing. If any of the students have begun to grow adult teeth (e.g., central incisors), have them circle these on the permanent teeth drawing. Use the transparency of this chart to show the most frequently missing teeth for the students. Place an X on those teeth on the transparency.

4. Show and discuss the transparency Inside a Tooth. Show the actual teeth specimens.

5. Show the teeth x-rays on the overhead projector. Point out the roots of the teeth which are hidden below the gum line and go deep into the jawbone. If any primary and adult teeth are on the x-rays, point these out to the students so they realize that the teeth they now have are mostly primary (baby) teeth which will be pushed out as the adult teeth grow into place.

Closure

Have a dentist or dental assistant visit the class to tell them about how their teeth grow and demonstrate how to care for their teeth.

A Look at My Teeth *(cont.)*

Here Are My Teeth

Name:_____ Date: _____

To the Student: Place an X over the teeth in the drawing which are missing from your mouth.

Permanent (Adult) Teeth
7–21 years of age

Primary (Baby) Teeth
8–33 months of age

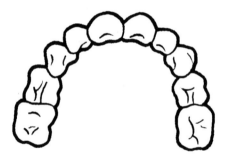

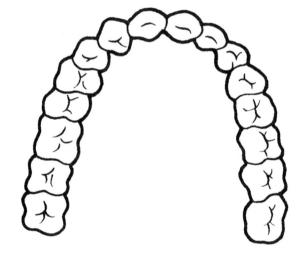

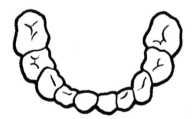

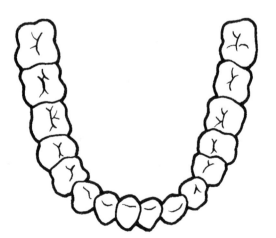

Inside a Tooth

The tooth is held tightly in the jawbone.

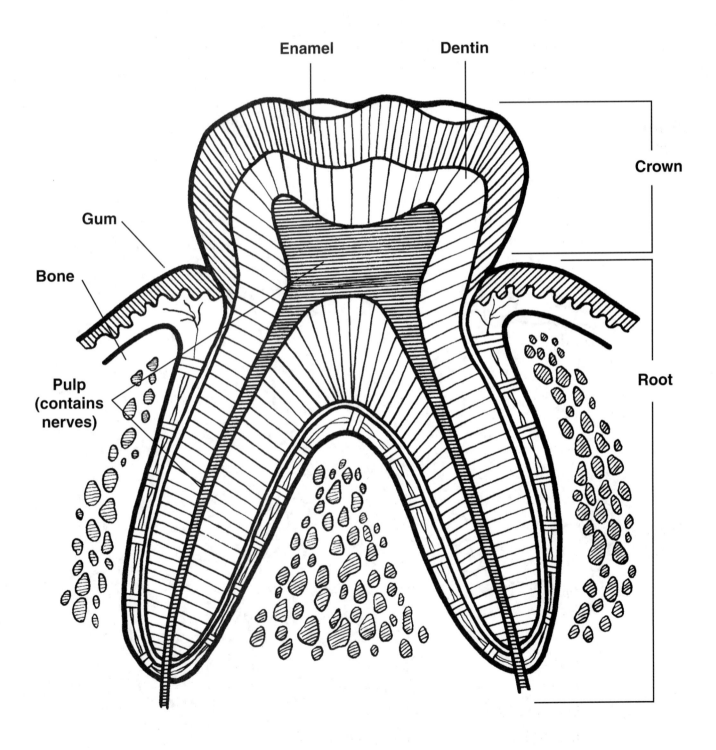

Sequence of Eruption of Teeth

central incisor	8–12 months	
lateral incisor	9–13 months	
cuspid	16–22 months	
first molar	13–19 months	
second molar	25–33 months	

Primary Teeth

second molar	23–31 months
first molar	14–18 months
cuspid	17–23 months
lateral incisor	10–16 months
central incisor	6–10 months

central incisor	7–8 years
lateral incisor	8–9 years
cuspid	11–12 years
first bicuspid	10–11 years
second bicuspid	10–12 years
first molar	6–7 years
second molar	12–13 years
third molar	17–21 years

Permanent Teeth

third molar	17–21 years
second molar	11–13 years
first molar	6–7 years
second bicuspid	11–12 years
first bicuspid	10–12 years
cuspid	9–10 years
lateral incisor	7–8 years
central incisor	6–7 years

Look Into My Eyes

Overview: *Students will investigate how their eyes work.*

Materials

- mirror for each student
- transparency of The Parts of the Eye (page 9)
- *optional:* cow eyes (These may be purchased through Carolina Biological Company. See page 48.)

Activity

1. Tell students that for several days they are going to try various tests to learn how the eyes work. Distribute a mirror to each student and explain that they are to look carefully at one eye. Pair them with other students to compare their eyes and discuss what they see. Discuss what students find as they examine their eyes. They should notice the following:

   - Colored ring and black circle in the center of the eye.

   - Most of the eye is white.

   - Tiny blood vessels may be seen (reassure them this is normal).

2. Have them close their eyes and gently feel the skull around the eyes to see how it protects the eye. Tell them to gently press on the eye to see what shape it is and if it is hard or soft. Explain that the eye is a ball shape but most of it is deep inside the skull to protect it. Tell them the eye is filled with fluid, like a water balloon, and thus feels somewhat hard.

3. Tell the students to look up, down, sideways, and then roll their eyes. Explain that muscles attached to the eyeball make it possible for this motion, just as other muscles move their legs and arms.

4. Explain that there is a hole in the center of the eye, covered by clear skin. Light enters the eye through this hole, and when it is dark, muscles enlarge the hole to let in more light. Explain that they will experiment to see the pupil change size.

5. Tell students to hold a mirror in front of one eye and look at the dark circle in the middle, the hole called the *pupil*. Tell them to continue to hold the mirror where it is and to close their eyes. They should then place a hand over both eyes to make it darker. Say that you are going to count to 10 very slowly and then they should take their hands away from their eyes and quickly look in the mirror at the hole. It may be necessary to repeat this several times for students to see the change in the pupil.

6. Show students the transparency of The Parts of the Eye. The full explanation of the functions of these parts is provided for teacher background. Students should not memorize the correct terms but, rather, have a basic understanding of their functions.

Closure

If appropriate for your students, dissect a cow's eye to show the parts. The skin of the eye is tough, so sharp cuticle scissors are suited for opening it and easier to control than a scalpel. The eye parts can be seen, including the pupil, lens, muscles, optic nerve, and the fluids which fill the eye. Use the transparency to show the location and name of the parts during the dissection.

Look Into My Eyes (cont.)

The Parts of the Eye

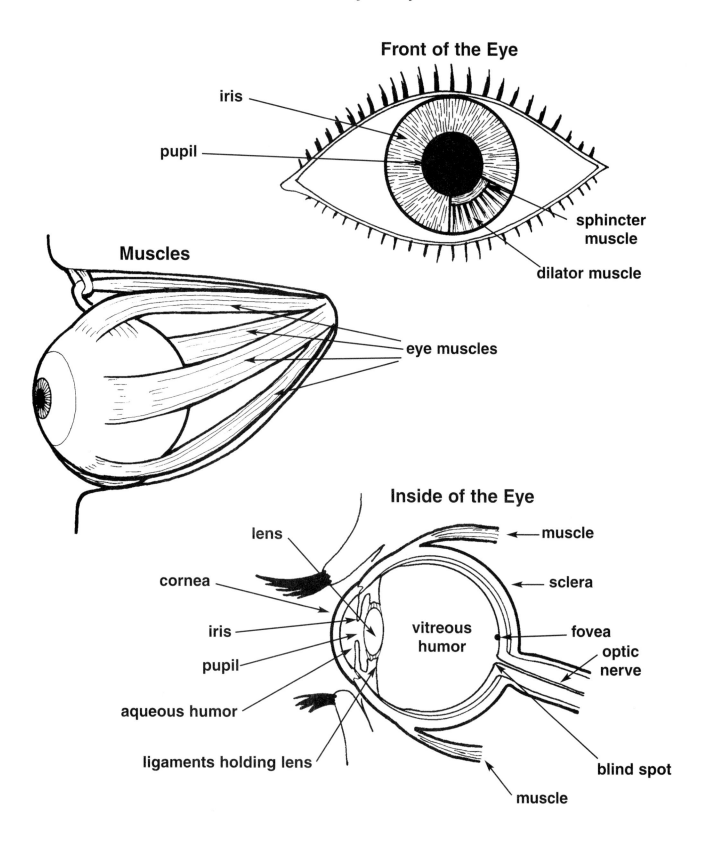

Front of the Eye

iris

pupil

sphincter muscle

dilator muscle

Muscles

eye muscles

Inside of the Eye

lens

cornea

iris

pupil

aqueous humor

ligaments holding lens

muscle

sclera

vitreous humor

fovea

optic nerve

blind spot

muscle

Look Into My Eyes *(cont.)*

Functions of Parts of the Eye

Note: This information is provided as teacher background. It defines the terms used on The Parts of the Eye diagrams. If appropriate, it may be shared with the students in a simplified form which they can understand.

Aqueous Humor: This is a clear watery fluid between the cornea and the pupil. It nourishes and lubricates the cornea and lens and fills the area between them.

Blind Spot: This is the area where the optic nerve leaves the retina. No vision cells are in this location, thus leaving a *hole* in what we see. This is so tiny that it does not affect the image we see.

Cornea: This is clear, tough tissue covering the front of the eye. It lets in light and does 80% of the image focusing.

Dilator Muscle: This enlarges the pupil in dim light.

Fovea: This is a dimple in the retina where light focuses after entering the lens. It is located directly opposite the lens. Cones are concentrated here, and vision is most acute.

Iris: This is a colored disk just under the cornea. Its color comes from melanin, just like our skin. The iris absorbs light. People with light-colored eyes are more sensitive to light.

Lens: This is a flexible structure about the size of an aspirin and shaped like a magnifying lens. The lens focuses 20% of the light after it passes through the cornea. Muscles (*ligaments*) surround the lens and pull or relax to adjust the thickness of the lens to focus and project an upside-down image on the retina.

Optic Nerve: This transmits the electrical impulses to the brain. The ability of the brain to interpret the image right-side up and in depth comes from experience that begins at a person's birth.

Pupil: This is a hole in the center of the iris. Light enters the eye here and is regulated by the size of the hole.

Retina: This is the innermost layer of the wall of the eyeball. It is as fragile as wet tissue paper. Light-sensitive cells (rods and cones) in the retina absorb light rays and change them into electrical signals.

Sclera: This is a tough leather-like skin covering about $\frac{5}{6}$ of the eyeball. The eyeball is about one inch (2.5 cm) in diameter.

Sphincter Muscle: This makes the pupil smaller in bright light. The pupil also becomes smaller when focused on nearby objects to create a sharper image. Six muscles surround the eyeball to move it. Both eyes move together.

Vitreous Humor: This is a clear jelly-like substance which gives the eyeball its spherical shape and holds the retina on the back of the eye.

Control Center—The Brain

Overview: *Students will do three activities to learn how the brain functions.*

Materials

- three bowls
- ice
- peppermint candy
- water
- lined paper and pencil

Lesson Preparation

Heat water and pour it into one bowl; place ice water in the second and room-temperature water in the third.

Activity #1

1. Show students bowls with hot and cold water in them. Ask them if they can tell by looking which bowl holds hot water and which cold. (*They can't tell by just looking.*) Ask them how they can tell the different temperatures of the water. (*Feel it.*) Have several students put a hand in each bowl to distinguish hot from cold. Discuss how their brains helped them know the temperatures.

2. Add a bowl of room-temperature water. Tell students that this water is between hot and cold. Call for a volunteer to place a left hand in the cold water and a right hand in the hot water. After about three minutes tell the child to remove the hands and put both into lukewarm water. Have the child tell if the water feels cold or hot. (*It feels cold to the hand which was just in hot water but hot to the hand just in cold water.*) Explain that sometimes the brain gets mixed signals and can get confused. In this case, the extremes in cold and hot water made the nerves in the hands more sensitive to a change to a moderate temperature.

Activity #2

1. Tell students that the brain relays information from all parts of our body by electrical impulses that travel to the brain or other sensors before we react. Have a student sit on a table with legs hanging over the edge without touching the floor. Explain that you are going to tap a knee to see what happens to the leg. Stretch out your hand, palm up, and gently tap on the soft tissue just below the kneecap. The leg should jerk. Repeat this on the other leg. Ask students how the child knew to jerk his or her knee since you didn't say to do that.

2. Explain that the nerves in the area below the kneecap feel the tap and send a message to the nerves in the spine. The message is immediately relayed to muscles which jerk the knee.

3. Have students make a large circle with their backs toward the center of the circle. The teacher should join the circle and have everyone hold hands. Explain that you are going to squeeze the hand of one of the students holding your hands. Tell them that when that child feels the squeeze, he or she should squeeze the child holding the other hand and so on until it gets back to you. Do not let the students know when you squeeze the child's hand. When you feel the squeeze, let the students know.

Control Center—The Brain *(cont.)*

Activity #2 *(cont.)*

4. Repeat this and time how long it takes for the squeeze to make its way around the circle. Divide the circle into two circles and have the students repeat the process, this time beginning with a designated child in each circle and beginning on your cue. This should take much less time. Relate that to the knee jerk by telling them that it would take far longer if the impulse had to be relayed through the brain than through a receptor in the spinal cord.

Activity #3

1. Distribute lined paper to each child and have each write his or her name 10 times. Now, have them write their names again, this time writing them backwards. After they have finished, ask them which was quicker for them. Ask them why they think it took less time to write their names forward than it did to write them backwards.

2. Explain that they have trained their brains to remember the order of the letters in their names so they don't have to spend time thinking about the order of each letter when writing their names forward. When they are writing the letters backward, the brain needs to take more time to think which letter comes next.

Closure

• Tell the students that their brains also control their senses. Remind them of the hot and cold water test they did which required the use of the sense of touch. Explain that they are going to test how this works with taste. Distribute a peppermint candy to each child. Tell them not to place it in their mouths until you tell them to do so. Explain that you will give them three signals (see below) and they are to respond to each of them.

   ✓ One clap—pinch the nose closed.

   ✓ Two claps—place the candy in the mouth.

   ✓ Three claps—let go of the nose and breathe through it.

• Ask the students what happened when they let go of their nose. (*They got a strong sense of the flavor of the candy.*) Explain that to taste the candy, the sense of smell is needed to help relay to the brain information which is added to the impulse arriving from nerve sensors on the tongue.

Muscle Power

Overview: *Students will learn about their muscles through activities and examples of muscles on a chicken leg.*

Materials

- a chicken leg with the skin and muscles attached (chilled until ready to use)
- single-edged razor blade
- mirror for each student

Activity #1

1. Ask all students to "make a muscle." Ask them what happened to their arms when they did this. (*The muscle on the upper arm bulged, and the lower arm bent up to touch the upper arm.*)

2. Tell them to do this again and use the other hand to feel the muscle on top of the upper arm. Have them tell what the muscle felt like as the lower arm was rising.

3. Have them repeat this but have them feel the muscle just under the upper arm. They should feel the muscle under the upper arm bone relax as the arm rises and stiffen as it stretches out.

4. Explain that muscles beneath the skin of the arm are working in pairs to raise or lower the arm. Top muscles contract (become tight) as the lower arm is raised, while the lower muscle relaxes. The opposite happens when they lower the arm.

5. Show students the chicken leg. Peel off the skin to reveal tendons and muscles. Bend the leg to show how the muscles contract and relax. Compare this to what students just did.

6. Have students open and close a fist, explaining that tendons attached to the finger bones are pulled by the muscles in the palm of the hand. On the chicken leg, show the tendons connected to muscles and the base of the leg. Explain that tendons tie muscles to bone. Carefully cut the tendons at the bone and bend the leg again. Discuss the difference without the muscles being held to the bone. Separate the muscle groups and then count them. Look for the large vessels which supply blood to the muscles.

7. Carefully cut between the thigh and drumstick to show the joint. Show the tough bands of ligaments (white sheets) and cartilage caps. Let students feel how smooth this is. Ask how it would feel if these were rough surfaces (*painful and difficult to move the joints*). Have them feel a finger joint and keep feeling it as they bend the finger. Can they feel the bone and tendons?

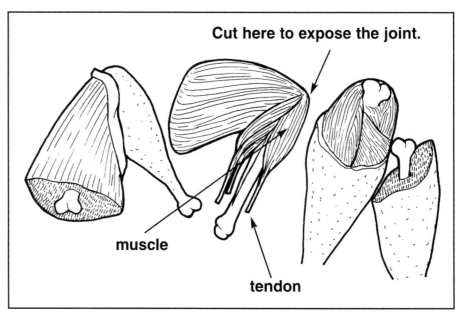

Cut here to expose the joint.

muscle

tendon

Activity #2

1. Explain that there are muscles beneath the skin in one's face to control facial expressions. Have them close their eyes and place their hands on their foreheads as they frown. Ask them to describe what they feel. (*The skin and muscles move.*)

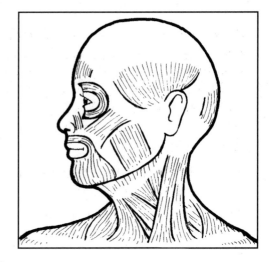

2. Distribute mirrors to students and tell them they are going to watch what happens as they use muscles in their faces. Tell them to do the following:

    ✓ Open and then close the nostrils.

    ✓ Raise and then lower the eyebrows.

    ✓ Raise and lower the ears.

    ✓ Wink one eye and then the other.

    ✓ Open the mouth as wide as possible and then close it.

    ✓ Stick out the tongue and then roll it.

    ✓ Push down the lower lip.

    ✓ Push up the lower lip.

    ✓ Turn the corners of the mouth up and then down.

    ✓ Make faces which show they are happy, sad, mad, and scared.

3. Discuss how they used their muscles to do all of this with their faces.

Closure

• Do this activity with the students so they can follow. Tell them each to sit in a chair some distance from their desks. Have them stand up. Ask them to repeat this and see how their thigh muscles feel as they rise. Discuss this so they realize that their bodies push forward and thigh muscles contract as they stand.

• Repeat this activity but this time have them fold their arms across their chests and stand while keeping their backs straight. Have them try again, checking to see if the thigh muscles are contracting. (*They are.*)

• Ask students what happens when they try to stand with arms folded. (*They can't stand.*)

• Ask what is different about the positions in the two experiments. (*They lean forward in the first but not in the second.*)

• Explain that gravity pulls us down, even when sitting. When we stand, we lean forward, shifting the pull of gravity over our feet. The thigh muscles contract and pull the legs to a standing position. If we keep the back straight, the pull of gravity is over the hips. The thigh muscles contract but can't pull hard enough against gravity to make us stand.

Dem Bones

Overview: *Students will learn about the bones in their bodies by examining those in owl pellets.*

Materials

- one-ounce plastic cups with lids
- trays (one per group)
- small cups of water
- tweezers
- toothpicks
- paper towels and newspaper
- one quart of water mixed with two tablespoons of bleach
- tea strainer
- colored construction paper

- copies of the Vole Skeleton (page 18) run on colored paper
- transparencies of Bone Identification Key, Vole Skeleton, and The Human Skeleton (pages 17–19)
- x-rays of human bones (Check with hospitals for these.)
- owl pellets, one for each group of two or three students (Owl pellets may be ordered from Genesis, Inc. See Resources section.)

Lesson Preparation

- Place the owl pellets in a flat container and add a small amount of water. Cover the container so moisture will be absorbed by the pellets and they will soften.

- Number the one-ounce cups, using a permanent marker. Assign a corresponding number to each student group.

- For each group, make up a tray containing the following:
    - ✓ newspaper and paper towels
    - ✓ one-ounce numbered cup and lid
    - ✓ softened owl pellet
    - ✓ pair of tweezers
    - ✓ toothpicks for each child
    - ✓ small cup of water

- Once the bones have been extracted from the pellet, they need to be cleaned and dried for use on the next day. This is done as follows:

    Cut four-inch (10 cm) newspaper squares and put the number which corresponds to each cup of bones on them. This will help to identify the bones as they are cleaned. Lay these on a tray.

Dem Bones *(cont.)*

Lesson Preparation *(cont.)*

Pour bleach mixture into each cup of bones and let sit at least an hour. Dump the contents into the tea strainer and rinse with clear water. Put bones on the newspaper with that group's number. Turn the cup upside down to dry overnight along with the bones. When the bones are dry, pour them back into the cups and put on lids.

Activity: Day One

1. Have students stand and remove shoes. As you lead them, have them feel the shape of bones in their fingers, arms, ribs, back, hips, legs, ankles, and toes. Show them the transparency of the human skeleton and x-rays of the human skeleton.

2. Tell them they are going to look at tiny bones which look very much like those in their bodies. Use the Teacher Information to explain the owl pellets and what they might find in them.

3. Divide students into pairs and distribute a tray of materials to each group. Explain that they are to pull the owl pellet into two or three parts to distribute among the group. Tell students to search the pellet, using fingers to feel for the bones. When bones are found, they should be placed in the small cup.

4. If skulls or other hollow bones are found, they may need to be dipped into water and washed. This is done by using tweezers to hold them and then picking out the fur with toothpicks.

5. When all bones are found, tell students that you will clean them so the next day they can find out just what they are.

Activity: Day Two

1. Divide students into their groups again and distribute the bones and a piece of dark construction paper. Tell them to sort the bones on the paper according to shape.

2. Use the transparency and x-rays to have them compare these bones with those of humans.

3. Use the transparency Bone Identification Key to help them recognize bones, especially skulls which identify the animals.

4. Select some bones to place on the Vole Skeleton transparency so students can see where they belong. Distribute a copy of this skeleton to each group and have them select bones which they can lay on the matching bones in the drawing.

5. Find a *femur* (leg bone) and a *pelvis* (hip bone) that match. Put the ball of the femur into the socket of the pelvis to show the joint. Use the overhead projector so all can see. Have students stand and place a hand on top of their leg where it joins the hip. Move the femur back and forth as they stand on one leg, feeling at the hip to sense the ball-and-socket joint moving.

Closure

Provide white glue, waxed paper, and toothpicks so each group can glue samples of bones to matching bones in the vole skeleton drawing. The glue will dry clear so the bones will be visible. Even the skull and jaw bone can be glued on the diagram. Place on cardboard, cover with plastic wrap, and display so students can compare the bones which have been found.

16

Bone Identification Key

	Voles and Rats	Mice	Shrews	Birds
Skull and Jaws	Teeth	Tooth	Tooth	No Teeth
Hips (pelvis)				
Shoulder (Scapula)	The shoulder blade is similar in all of these animals.			
Other	Mole Skull and Jaw	Beetle Wings / Insect Leg	Fish Bones / Scales	Bird Breastbone / Wing Bone

Dem Bones *(cont.)*

Vole Skeleton

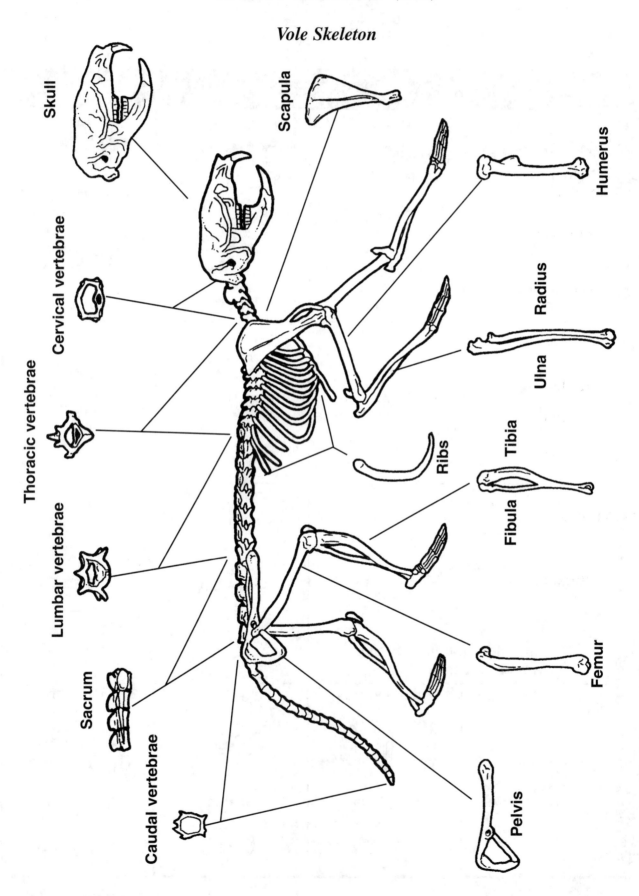

Skull

Scapula

Humerus

Cervical vertebrae

Radius

Thoracic vertebrae

Ulna

Lumbar vertebrae

Ribs

Tibia

Fibula

Femur

Sacrum

Caudal vertebrae

Pelvis

Dem Bones *(cont.)*

The Human Skeleton

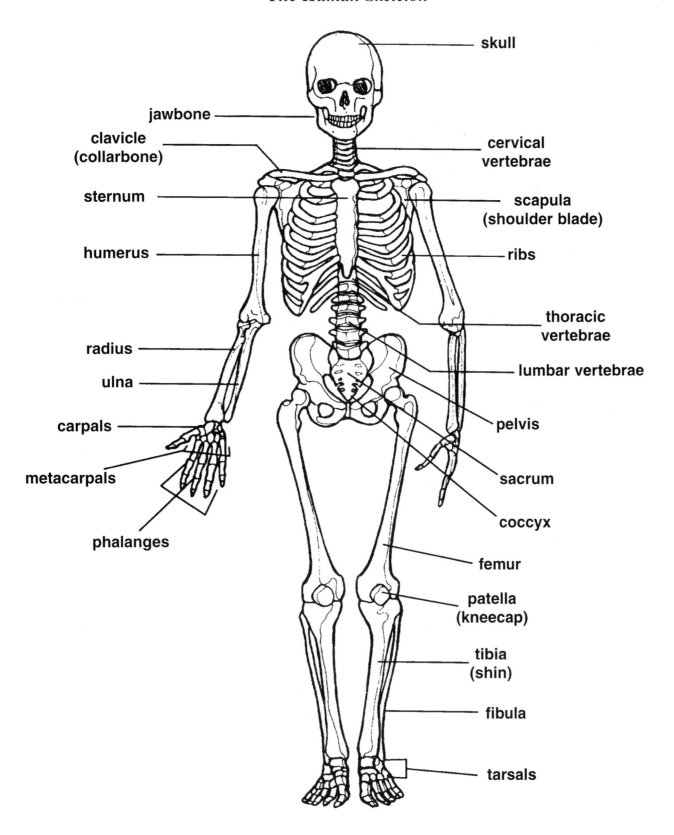

skull

jawbone

clavicle
(collarbone)

sternum

humerus

radius

ulna

carpals

metacarpals

phalanges

cervical
vertebrae

scapula
(shoulder blade)

ribs

thoracic
vertebrae

lumbar vertebrae

pelvis

sacrum

coccyx

femur

patella
(kneecap)

tibia
(shin)

fibula

tarsals

How Do We Breathe

Overview: *Students will learn how their lungs work and make a model of the lungs.*

Materials per Child

- one pint (.5 liter) clear plastic drinking-water bottles
- round balloon
- rubber band
- pint or quart-size clear plastic bag (Cut off any self-sealing edges.)

Other Materials

- transparency of How You Breathe (page 22)
- scissors

Lesson Preparation

- Cut off the bottom of the water bottle about two inches (5 cm) from the bottom.
- Make a model of the lung as described in #3 below so students will know what their finished product should look like.

Activity

1. Tell students to take a deep breath and then slowly exhale. Ask them what parts of their body they used to do this. (Most will say their mouth or nose and lungs.) Ask them to show you how large they think their lungs are. Demonstrate how to place one hand on the collar bone and the other at the bottom of the ribs. Explain that is the length of their lungs and that there are two of them, one on either side of the chest. Tell them that the lungs fill the chest cavity and are therefore quite large.

2. Tell students you want them to feel what happens when they breathe. The teacher should demonstrate for students so they can follow. Sit straight on a chair without pressing the back against the chair. Point flattened fingers of each hand down and place them just below the breastbone. As you breathe deeply through the mouth, press gently to feel movement up and down. This is the diaphragm, a muscle beneath the lungs. Have students run in place for a minute and then repeat this. They will feel the diaphragm moving higher into the chest as they breathe deeper.

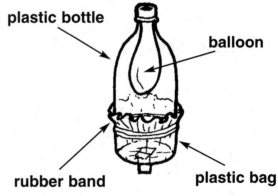

plastic bottle

balloon

rubber band

plastic bag

3. Tell students they will make a model of the lungs. Distribute a water bottle and balloon to each. Show your finished model as an example of what theirs will look like. Have them put the balloon into the mouth of the bottle and turn the edge of the balloon over the lip of the bottle to hold it in place. Put the plastic bag over the bottom of the bottle and secure it with the rubber band (or clear packing tape). Leave some of the bag hanging so it acts as a handle that lets you push and pull the bag.

How Do We Breathe? *(cont.)*

Activity *(cont.)*

4. Let students "play" with their models by pushing air in and out of the balloon, using the plastic bag. Explain that the balloon is like a lung but a real lung is not hollow like the balloon. A lung would look like a sponge, full of tiny air sacs. Tell them the plastic bag is the diaphragm which is a muscle in our body that pulls air into the lungs and pushes it out again.

Closure

- Show the transparency of How You Breathe and have the students pull down on the bag and watch the balloon inflate. Point to the diagram showing the person breathing in and the diaphragm being down. As they push the plastic bag up, the air is forced out of the balloon. Point to the next drawing showing the breathing-out position of the diaphragm. Have them notice that when the bag is pulled down, there is more space inside the bottle than when it is pushed up. Point out that this can be seen in the diagrams of the chest cavity also. The diaphragm pushes up, and the chest cavity becomes smaller so the air is pushed out of the lungs. When the diaphragm drops, it makes the space in the chest bigger and air is pulled into the lungs.

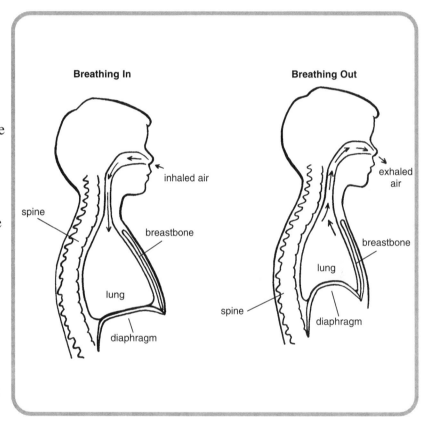

- Tell the students to put the opening of the balloon near their faces so they can feel the air rushing out when they push up on the bag.

- As they pull down on the bag, have the students take a deep breath to feel what is happening to their lungs. As they push the bag up, tell them to breathe out and feel the diaphragm doing its work for them. Have them repeat this several times as they use their lung model and their own lungs to breathe in and out.

How Do We Breathe? *(cont.)*

How You Breathe

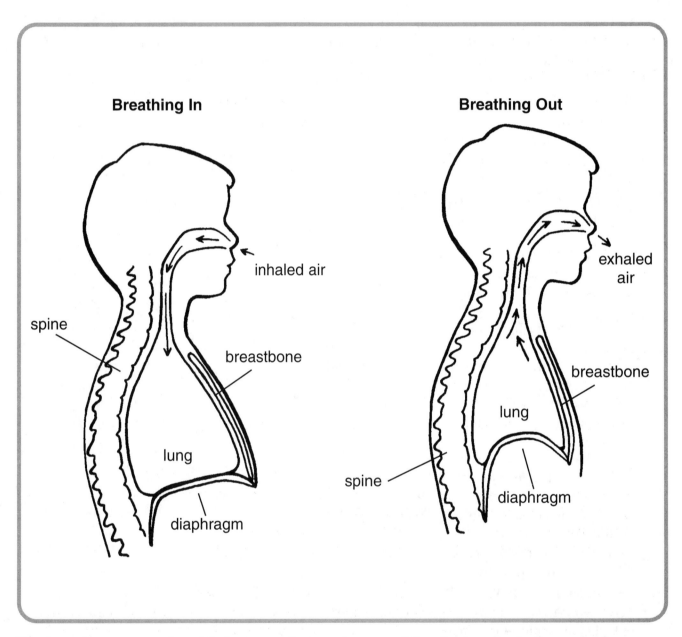

The lungs have no muscles of their own so the muscles around the chest cavity do the work of breathing. The *diaphragm* is a sheet of muscle stretching from the backbone to the front of the rib cage. It forms a moveable floor under the lungs. In quiet breathing it moves less than an inch. When you are breathing hard after exercise, it can move several inches up and down.

When the diaphragm contracts, the chest cavity becomes larger and the air pressure on the lungs is less. The outside air rushes in to equalize this pressure. When the diaphragm relaxes and moves up, the chest cavity is less and the air pressure is greater. Some of the air in the lungs now rushes out. During quiet breathing, the air entering your lungs is a gentle breeze moving about four miles (6.4 km) per hour.

How Do We Breathe? *(cont.)*

Take a Deep Breath

Overview: *Students will learn more about the structure of the lungs and experiment to measure the amount of air in their lungs.*

Materials

- bubble solution
- drinking straws
- rulers
- transparency of The Lungs (page 25)
- transparency of Graph of Air Exhaled from the Lungs (page 26)

- large soft sponge
- large clear container of water
- 3" x 5" (8 cm x 13 cm) lined file cards
- trays (*optional:* sheets of waxed paper)

Lesson Preparation

- For each group prepare a tray of materials: a container of bubble solution, straws, file cards for each member, and a ruler.
- This activity must be done indoors to prevent the wind from breaking the bubbles.

Activity

1. Have students use the lung models to tell what they have learned about lungs and how much air their lungs will hold.

2. Use the transparency The Lungs to show students what their lungs look like and learn more about their function.

3. Show students the sponge and explain that lungs look much like a sponge. Pass the sponge around so students can see how light it is. Cut it in half to show that the holes are throughout the sponge. Let students know that these are really air sacs in the sponge, not holes, and that their lungs have these as well. Place one half the sponge in the water and let them see that it floats until water enters the air sacs, forces out the air, and makes the sponge so heavy that it begins to sink.

4. Tell students that they are going to see how much air their lungs can hold. Divide students into small groups and give each group a tray of bubble materials. Let each student write his or her name on a file card and then write **1**, **2**, and **3** at the beginning of the first three lines. Have them remove all items from the tray and pour about a tablespoon (15 mL) of bubble solution on the tray. They should spread it around with their hands to make the entire surface wet with the solution.

5. Show them how to dip one end of a straw into the bubble solution and blow a bubble through it. After they have been successful, show them how to take a very deep breath and this time blow the biggest bubble they can on the surface of the tray. When the bubble pops, use a ruler to measure its diameter and write it on a file card. Do this until three trials have been completed. Tell all the group members to take turns blowing one bubble and then repeat this until three trials have been made.

Take a Deep Breath (cont.)

Closure

- Tell the students to circle the measurement of the largest bubble they blew. Use this data to help students see how to construct a graph. Distribute a small self-adhesive note to each student and have each write his or her name and bubble size on it.

- Ask the students to tell you their bubble sizes. Find the largest and smallest bubbles. Project the transparency of the Graph of Air Exhaled from the Lungs on the board. Write the bubble sizes in order from smallest to largest on the horizontal axis.

- Have each student place his or her note on the line which represents the size of that bubble. Ask the students to help you count the notes for each measurement and then complete the vertical axis.

- Let students have the experience of analyzing this data by asking them the following:

  ✓ What was the largest bubble size?

  ✓ What was the smallest bubble size?

  ✓ What was the size of the bubble most of the students blew? (Explain that this was the average-size bubble for the class.)

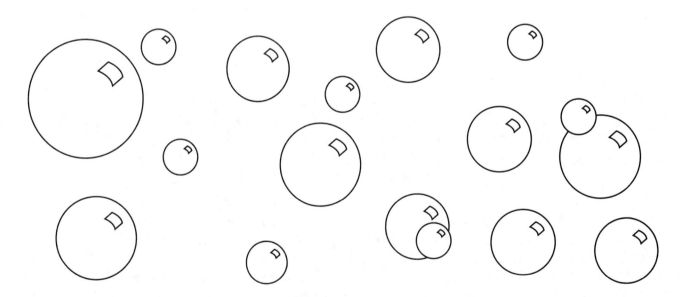

- Tell the students your largest bubble size and compare it with the size of theirs. (*The teacher's bubble should be larger.*) Find the bubble measurements for the tallest students in the class and see if they blew larger bubbles than the shortest students.

- Explain to the students that our lungs grow as we grow and the bigger we are, the larger our lungs become. Therefore, if their lungs did not hold as much air as someone else's did, they may have smaller lungs. Tell them also that we can never squeeze out all the air in our lungs.

How Do We Breathe? *(cont.)*

The Lungs

The respiratory center in the brain stem controls the diaphragm, telling it how fast to pull in air. It tells the heart to beat faster if you need more oxygen. It does this automatically.

The tubes leading into the lungs look like an upside down tree. Air comes in through the nose or mouth into the windpipe (*trachea*), which branches into two main tubes (*bronchi*). These continue to divide into smaller and smaller branches until they reach the tiny air sacs (*alveoli*).

Your lungs contain hundreds of millions of tiny air sacs (*alveoli*). Tubes no thicker than a hair carry blood cells past the air sacs. Carbon dioxide gas collected by the blood cells from your body passes through the walls of these tubes, and oxygen passes out of the sacs and into the blood cells. These blood cells return to the heart and take blood to all parts of the body.

When you breathe, a trapdoor (*epiglottis*) which is attached to the root of your tongue allows air to enter the trachea. When you swallow, the epiglottis closes over the trachea so no food can get into your lungs. If food does get past this trapdoor, it can be forced out by pressing hard under the diaphragm so it pops out.

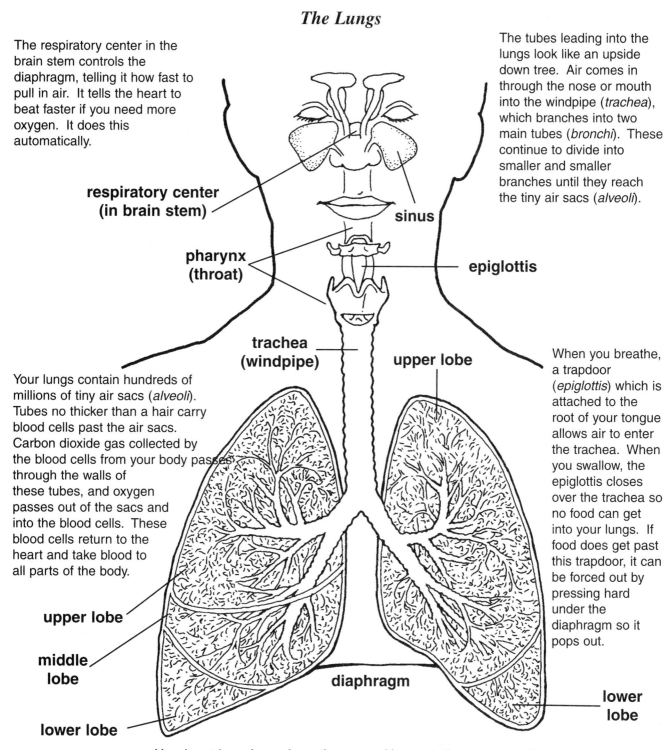

respiratory center (in brain stem)

sinus

pharynx (throat)

epiglottis

trachea (windpipe)

upper lobe

upper lobe

middle lobe

lower lobe

diaphragm

lower lobe

Your heart is under and mostly centered between the two lungs. Your right lung has three lobes, each with its own section of the bronchial tree. Your left lung has only two lobes, with a notch to fit the bottom of your heart. If one lobe is damaged, the others keep functioning. Healthy people do not use their entire lung capacity, and so they have extra breathing power. You exhale only about $\frac{1}{6}$ of the air in your lungs. That means most of the air is left in your lungs.

How Do We Breathe? *(cont.)*

Graph of Air Exhaled from the Lungs

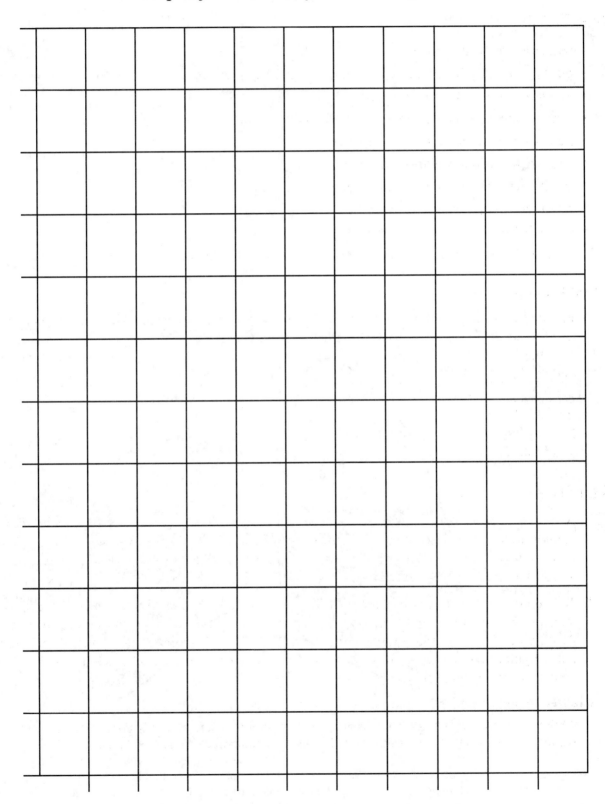

Number of Students

Bubble Diameters

This is Your Heart

Overview: *Students will learn how their heart functions through a series of activities.*

Materials

- regular-sized white bedsheet
- black, maroon, red, and pink permanent felt markers
- maroon and red construction paper
- stethoscopes (cardboard tubes will work but not as well)
- transparency of Diagram of the Heart and Lungs (page 29)
- copy of The Blood Cell's Journey (page 30)
- small juice boxes with red drink (one per student)
- small paper cups (one per student)
- tennis balls
- picture of the circulatory system of the human body (See Resources section.)

Lesson Preparation

- Pin the bedsheet to a wall and project the transparency of the Diagram of the Heart and Lungs on it, making it as large as possible. Trace the drawing with pencil. Lay it on a table and trace over the lines with permanent felt pen. Trace the veins leading into the heart (the right atrium and ventricle) and the arteries leading right and left into the lungs (see arrows) in purple or maroon pen. Trace all other parts of the heart in red. Outline the lungs in pink. Use black to trace the captions.

- Cut out ovals about three inches (7.5 cm) long and nearly circular from the construction paper to represent blood cells.

Activity #1

1. Ask the students if they have ever been cut. Have them tell you what color their blood was. Tell them to look at the veins in their wrists and hands and tell what color they see. (*Most will say they see blue.*) Explain that this is blood flowing through their wrists and hands, and although it looks blue, it is really a dark purple.

2. Tell students that you want them to do an experiment. Have them raise one arm straight up above their heads and let the other hang straight down. They should hold this position for one minute. At the end of the time, have them compare the hands. They should see that the one held high is much lighter than the other. It will also feel slightly colder than the other hand. Ask them to explain what was happening. (*Do not correct them if they offer wrong ideas.*)

3. Give students unlined paper and have them draw how they think blood travels through their bodies. (*This is a check of their level of understanding, so do not give any answers.*) Have students share some of the ideas with the class or in small groups.

This is Your Heart *(cont.)*

Activity #1 *(cont.)*

4. Explain that the heart is a muscle which pumps blood throughout the body. Tell them that they are going to make a heart from a juice container. Distribute a juice container and a cup to each child. Help them push the straw into the container. Tell them the container is the heart and the straw is the artery leading from the heart. Have them squeeze the container and watch the drink flow into the cup. Explain the red drink is like their blood. Let them continue squeezing the container, forcing the juice into the cup.

5. Tell students that the heart muscle is actually harder to squeeze than the container. Divide the students in small groups and give each group a tennis ball. Have them squeeze the ball and explain that this is how hard it is for their hearts to pump blood through their bodies.

6. Let the students listen to another student's heart through the stethoscope. This needs to be done in a quiet room.

Activity #2

1. Tell students that they are going to take a trip through the heart. Place the bedsheet with the heart on the floor. Have students gather around it so you can explain the parts of the heart. Point out that they are looking down on the heart so the left and right sides are reversed.

2. Select three students to help with the demonstration of blood traveling through the heart. Two will be stationed in each of the lungs and will hold red blood cells. The third will carry a maroon blood cell and stand at the *inferior vena cava* ready to enter the heart. They represent blood and will follow the arrows moving through the heart as directed by the script you read aloud.

3. Begin to read The Blood Cell's Journey and help the student with the maroon blood cell move along toward the lungs. The blood cells should each go to the left lung, where they exchange their maroon blood cell for a red one and then reenter the heart on the other side. Finally, they exit the heart to the upper or lower body.

4. Let other students take this journey so they can see how their blood travels through their heart and lungs and out into their bodies. They may enter from above or below the heart and go to either lung before going to the other side of the heart. They can leave the heart to pass to the upper or lower body.

5. Show the students a picture of the circulatory system in the body so they can see how the blood travels from the heart throughout their bodies.

Closure

Return the drawings students made earlier about how blood passes through their bodies and let them make another drawing to show what they have learned.

Diagram of the Heart and Lungs

Left Lung

Air sacs (alveoli)

Capillaries

Pulmonary Veins

Pulmonary Artery

Aorta

To upper body

From left lung

Left ventricle

Right ventricle

Left atrium

From upper body

To right lung

Right atrium

Inferior vena cava

To lower body

From lower body

Right Lung

The Blood Cell's Journey (Script)

You are a blood cell just entering the heart from below the heart. The blood pressure has forced you on your journey all the way through this body to the heart. You are dull red (maroon) in color now since you don't have much oxygen but a lot of carbon dioxide that you picked up from cells along your way. You moved faster as you got nearer the heart, and now you are swept into the . . .

Inferior Vena Cava, a large vein which lets all blood return from the lower body. The heart relaxes and blood rushes into the . . .

Right Atrium. Now you find yourself in a small pocket which has a white bulging floor made of three triangular flaps of a valve which suddenly spring open, pouring you into the . . .

Right Ventricle. This is a large chamber in the lower right side of the heart. Just when you thought you were safe, there is a loud BOOM as the heart beats, squeezing this chamber hard. You go racing up through a valve into the . . .

Pulmonary Artery. This tube leads into the left and right lungs. You are forced into the left lung where this tube narrows into thin capillaries again. You join the line of blood cells in single file, passing through the thin walls of the . . .

Alveoli. These microscopic air sacs make up the sponge-like lungs, which are filled every time you breathe in. Our air has many different gases in it. About $1/5$ of it is the gas oxygen. You give off the carbon dioxide gas molecules and take oxygen molecules through the alveoli walls, which are much thinner than tissue paper. (*The blood cell exchanges the maroon cell for a bright red one.*) The lungs will exhale the carbon dioxide and bring in fresh air with oxygen in it.

This journey isn't over yet! You now flow into the pulmonary vein. As the heart relaxes, you flow into the . . .

Left Atrium, located in the upper left part of the heart. The atrium is a small sack that fills with blood cells as the heart relaxes. It waits for a split second for the valves below to open, and then the blood cell pours into the lower chamber, called the . . .

Left Ventricle. The blood doesn't stay in this chamber long either. Once again, the heart squeezes (beats), forcing the blood cells through the valve in the top of this chamber and into the thick walled tube called the . . .

Aorta. This thick tube splits into three large arteries. Some blood flows to the upper body, going to the arms, fingertips, and the brain. The rest of the blood goes to the lower body, traveling all the way to the tips of the toes.

Your blood circulates everywhere, including the kidneys, brain, and the heart itself. It removes wastes from the body and carries nutrients and oxygen to all your cells. What wonderful life-giving "juice" your blood is! You can help it do its job by eating healthy food and getting plenty of exercise every day to keep your body in good shape.

Where Does Food Go?

Overview: *Students will take a walk through the digestive system to see how food passes through the body.*

Materials

- twin-size white bedsheet
- transparency of The Digestive System (page 32)
- copy of Food Travelogue (page 33)
- various colored permanent pens
- measuring tape
- string and thick yarn

Lesson Preparation

- Pin the bedsheet to a wall and project the transparency of The Digestive System. Trace the picture with pencil and then lay the sheet on a table. Trace over drawing and labels with colored felt pens.
- Cut a length of string eight yards (7.2 meters) long. Measure two yards (1.8 meters) of thick yarn. Use tape to label it the "Large Intestine." Tape the yarn to the string and measure seven yards (6.3 meters) from where they join. This part is to be labeled "Small Intestine." The remaining string is the distance from the mouth through the stomach and into the small intestine.

Activity

1. Conduct this lesson following lunch. Give each child unlined paper to draw where they think their lunch goes after it is swallowed. Have them begin their drawings at the mouth and show its journey to the point where it leaves the body. (*Do not give any information since this is a pretest.*)

2. Tell students they will journey through the digestive system to follow food through the body. Lay the bedsheet on the floor to see the parts of the digestive system. Ask for a volunteer to walk through the body as you read the script. The underlined terms in the script are the labels found on the drawing. Point these out as the student moves through the digestive system.

3. Ask students how long they think the entire digestive system is from mouth to anus in an adult. Say you are going to walk from the front of the room and they are to hold up a hand when they think you have gone as far as the digestive system would stretch. Begin moving slowly and stop when most hands are up.

4. Let a volunteer hold the "mouth" end of the string and begin to stretch it out. Stop to show the distance to the stomach and then the small intestine. Let students update predictions on the length of the digestive system by having a volunteer stand at the point they think you will reach when all string is unwound. Unwind the string and show students the full length of the system. Explain that this is what would be found inside a six-foot person; their digestive systems would be shorter since they are smaller.

5. Have them look at the small and large intestine and explain how they got their names. (*The small intestine is longer but thinner than the large intestine.*)

Closure

Distribute students' original drawings of the digestive system and let them draw another.

Where Does Food Go? *(cont.)*

The Digestive System

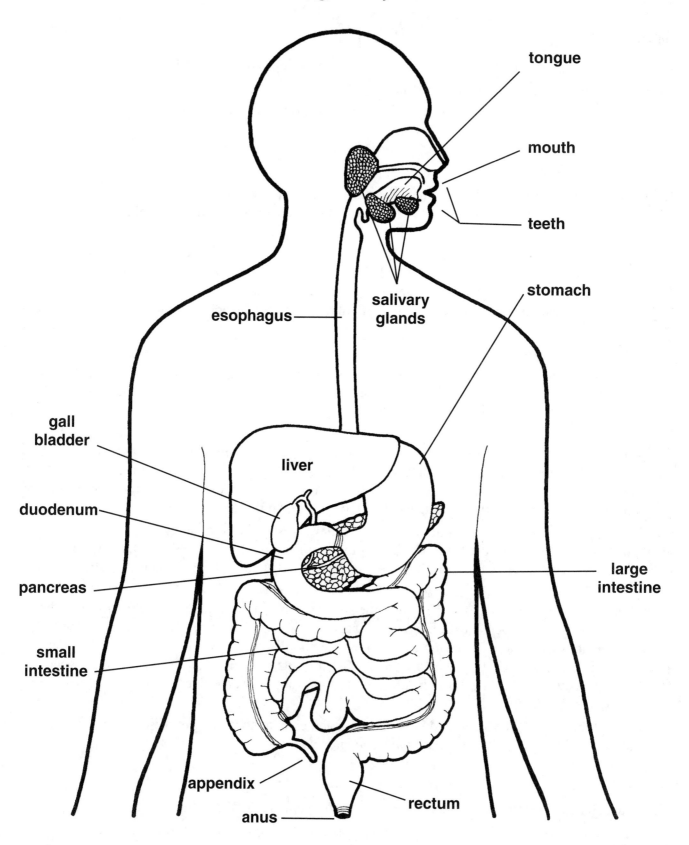

tongue

mouth

teeth

salivary
glands

esophagus

stomach

gall
bladder

liver

duodenum

pancreas

large
intestine

small
intestine

appendix

rectum

anus

Where Does Food Go? *(cont.)*

Food Travelogue

The tongue and teeth work together, breaking food apart and pushing it around. Saliva pours into the mouth from salivary glands to begin digesting food, softening and lubricating it on its way. The tongue pushes against the roof of the mouth as you swallow, helping push food down the . . .

Esophagus, which is about 10 inches (25.4 cm) long in an adult. It lies behind your windpipe (trachea) and is flattened when empty. As you swallow, you stop breathing for a moment. A trapdoor called the epiglottis automatically closes the opening to your voice box and lungs, and the soft palate at the back of the roof of your mouth swings up to shut off the passage to your nose. If you swallow too fast, the epiglottis may not have time to close, causing you to cough to clear out any food that might enter the trachea. The muscles in the esophagus ripple to push the food into the . . .

Stomach, where gastric juices made of hydrochloric acid and the enzyme pepsin are released to break down protein in food. These acids are strong enough to eat through the wall of the stomach. Normally, these acids are not manufactured until food is in the stomach and a protective mucus coats the stomach. Like a balloon, the stomach expands with food. The muscles which surround it begin to churn the food back and forth. Carbohydrates move out first and then proteins. Fats are the last to leave the stomach. Some food may remain in the stomach for two to five hours. The food is now called *chyme*; it is a thick liquid. The chyme squeezes into the . . .

Duodenum, the first 10 inches of the small intestine where the digestive process will be completed by other juices. Like a large salivary gland, the pancreas produces pancreatic juice. One to two pints (.5–1 liter) of pancreatic juice per day pour into the duodenum to digest carbohydrates, proteins, and fats. Bile is made by the liver and stored in the gall bladder. Bile works like a detergent to break down fats so they can be dissolved in water and absorbed into the body. Pancreatic juices and bile flow into the duodenum through the bile duct. The partly digested food now moves into the . . .

Small Intestine where about five pints (2.1 liters) of digestive juices enter through the walls daily. Completely digested food has been changed to nutrients which can now be absorbed through tiny fingers (*villi*) that line the walls of the small intestine. Tiny blood and lymph vessels are inside the villi. They take in the vitamins, minerals, and other nutrients and carry them to all parts of the body through the blood and lymph systems. The average adult absorbs about 10 quarts (9 liters) of digested food and liquid each day. The journey through the small intestine may take four to eight hours. What remains undigested passes into the . . .

Large Intestine where it spends 10 to 12 hours losing large quantities of water and nutrients. At the end, the solution is fed on by a colony of bacteria which decay the remains (feces). The feces are brown because they contain dead blood cells. What is left of your meal passes to the rectum, ready to leave the body through the opening called the anus. The entire journey lasts about 15 to 48 hours.

Moving Out

Overview: *Students will simulate the movement of food through the intestines.*

Materials

- one pair of pantyhose
- one banana
- one plastic bag
- transparent packing tape
- green food coloring
- two tablespoons (30 mL) of water
- *Your Insides* by Joanna Cole

Lesson Preparation

- Cut the pantyhose in half; only one leg of the hose will be used. Cut off the toe of the hose.
- Mix the food coloring and water.

Activity

1. Review the steps of the journey through the digestive system which students took during the previous activity. Tell them that they are going to see what happens when food has passed out of the stomach and into the intestines.

2. Hold up the banana and explain that it will be the food they have just eaten. Peel it and place it in a plastic bag. Add the colored water and tell them this will be the gastic juices from the stomach. Roll the bag around the banana and seal it with tape. Be sure to squeeze all the air out of the bag and wrap the tape around the bag to strengthen it. Mash the banana slightly to simulate the stomach muscles squeezing it.

3. Show the students the panty hose and explain that it represents the intestines. Have them line up in a double line, facing a partner. Give them the pantyhose to stretch out and hold. Place the bagged banana inside the top end of the pantyhose. Show the students how to use their hands to massage the banana on its way through the hose. Each child should give the banana a squeeze to keep it moving and to mash it further. Continue moving the banana along until it reaches the toe of the pantyhose. Take the banana out of the bag and unwrap it to show your children the "digested" banana.

Closure

Read aloud *Your Insides* or similar literature about the digestive system.

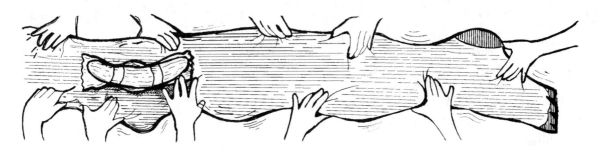

Nutrition and You

Overview: *Students will learn how to choose nutritional foods for good health.*

Materials

- empty food packages and cans
- nutritional charts from fast food restaurants
- transparency of the Nutritional Facts chart (page 36)
- copies and a transparency of What Your Body Needs To Be Healthy (page 39)
- copies of the Breakfast Chart (page 38)
- enlarged copy of the Daily Food Guide (page 43)
- copies of Healthy You Puzzle (pages 40–42), reproduced on tag board
- copies of My Product Chart (page 37)

Lesson Preparation

- Cut out the puzzle piece circles (pages 40–42) and then cut them into thirds. Place each set in an envelope to be used by student groups. (See Activity 3.)
- Gather nutritional charts from assorted fast food restaurants.
- Post the enlarged copy of the Daily Food Guide on the bulletin board. Invite students to bring in pictures of these foods and place them around the chart.

Activity #1

1. Show the transparency of Nutritional Facts to the students and discuss it with them. Tell them that they will be doing activities that will help them make choices of the best food to eat in order to stay healthy. Divide the students into small groups and distribute the My Product Chart (page 37) to each student. Provide each group with assorted food packages and cans. Let each student select one of these and then copy the nutritional information on their chart. Discuss the results with the students.

2. Distribute a copy of the breakfast chart on page 38 to each student for homework. Tell students to complete this form, using their next breakfast, and bring it back to class the next day. (*Suggestion*: Attach a note to the parents explaining the purpose of this activity.) Review the completed charts in class to compare what students eat for breakfast.

3. Divide the students into small groups and distribute an envelope of puzzle pieces to each of them. Provide each group with a copy of the What Your Body Needs To Be Healthy chart (page 39). Tell the students to shuffle the game pieces and then deal them out to the members of their group. Have the students lay out the **A** pieces and then begin to match **B** and **C** pieces to each of these, using the chart as a guide. Use a transparency of the chart to discuss what they learned in this game.

4. Divide the students into groups and distribute a copy of the Eating for Good Health (page 43), Making Healthy Choice chart (page 44) and the What Your Body Needs To Be Healthy chart (page 39). They will also need a copy of one of the completed breakfast charts (page 38). Provide each group with a different fast food nutritional chart. Tell them to select three items that will make up their lunch and copy the nutritional information on to their chart. Have each group transfer the information from their breakfast and lunch charts to the How Healthy Is Your Diet? chart (page 45) to calculate the total nutrients.

Closure

- Discuss what students learned about making healthy choices at fast food restaurants.
- Have the students write a brief essay to explain how they may need to change what they eat to stay healthy.

Nutrition and You *(cont.)*

Nutritional Facts

Serving Size

This is an average portion. Compare this to the amount you really eat. Eating twice as much means twice the calories and nutrients.

Calories

Your body burns calories for energy. You need about 2,200 per day. Look for foods with the fewest calories from fat.

% Daily Value

This is the percent of your day's recommended total of a particular nutrient. It is based on a 2,000 per day calorie diet.

Total Fat

The fewer grams (g), the better. Aim for under 65 grams a day. Saturated fat should be less than 1/2 the total grams of fat.

Cholesterol

High cholesterol can lead to heart disease. The less cholesterol, the better. Aim for less than 300 milligrams (mg) per day.

Salt

This is salt, and the less you eat, the better. Eat 2,400 mg or less per day.

Total Carbohydrates

The total carbohydrates and dietary fiber you eat daily should be high (no less than 300 g per day). Keep your sugar intake low.

Protein

You need about 45–60 g per day.

Minerals and Vitamins

You need small amount of these daily

- calcium (800–1,200 mg)
- iron (10–12 mg)
- vitamin C (45 mg)
- vitamin B1 (1mg)
- vitamin B2 (1 mg)

Nutrition and You *(cont.)*

My Product Chart

Serving Size Servings per Container		
Calories Per Serving Fat Calories		
Per Serving	**Amount**	**% Daily Value**
Total Fat		
Saturated Fat		
Cholesterol		
Sodium		
Total Carbohydrate		
Protein		
Sugars		
Vitamin C		
Vitamin B_1		
Vitamin B_2		
Calcium		
Iron		

Nutrition and You *(cont.)*

Breakfast Chart

Save this menu. You will need it for the activities on pages 44 and 45.

Nutrients	Mass Daily Value		Mass Daily Value		Mass Daily Value	
	Cereal:_____ Serving Size:_____		Milk (type): _____ Serving Size:_____		Juice (type): _____ Serving Size:_____	
Calories	_____		_____		_____	
Calories from fat	_____		_____		_____	
Fat	_____g	_____%	_____g	_____%	_____g	_____%
Saturated Fat	_____g	_____%	_____g	_____%	_____g	_____%
Cholesterol	_____mg	_____%	_____mg	_____%	_____mg	_____%
Sodium	_____mg	_____%	_____mg	_____%	_____mg	_____%
Potassium	_____mg	_____%	_____mg	_____%	_____mg	_____%
Total Carbohydrate	_____g	_____%	_____g	_____%	_____g	_____%
Dietary Fiber	_____g	_____%	_____g	_____%	_____g	_____%
Sugars	_____g	_____%	_____g	_____%	_____g	_____%
Protein	_____g	_____%	_____g	_____%	_____g	_____%
Vitamin A	_____mg	_____%	_____mg	_____%	_____mg	_____%
Vitamin C	_____mg	_____%	_____mg	_____%	_____mg	_____%
Calcium	_____mg	_____%	_____mg	_____%	_____mg	_____%
Iron	_____mg	_____%	_____mg	_____%		
Vitamin D	_____mg	_____%	_____mg	_____%		
Vitamin E	_____mg	_____%				
Thiamine	_____mg	_____%				
Riboflavin	_____mg	_____%				
Niacin	_____mg	_____%				
Vitamin B$_6$	_____mg	_____%				
Folate	_____mg	_____%				
Vitamin B$_{12}$	_____mg	_____%				
Phosphorus	_____mg	_____%				
Magnesium	_____mg	_____%				
Zinc	_____mg	_____%				
Copper	_____mg	_____%				

My Breakfast Menu

Your Daily Values

You should eat about 2,200 calories per day. The nutrients you need are shown below:

Total Fat	Less than 65 g
Saturated Fats	Less than 20 g
Cholesterol	Less than 300 mg
Sodium	Less than 2,400 mg
Total Carbohydrates	300 g
Dietary Fiber	25 g

1 gram (g) = 1,000 milligrams (mg)

Nutrition and You (cont.)

What Your Body Needs To Be Healthy

Nutrients	What They Do For You	Best Source
Water	This is an extremely important nutrient. You can go without water for only about a week. Your body needs water to dissolve nutrients and carry them to your cells, to carry wastes from your body, and to cool you.	water and liquid
Fats	Fats are a highly concentrated source of energy. Each gram of fat is about 9 calories, which are burned by your body to give you energy.	dairy products, butter, and fatty red meat
Proteins	You eat food with proteins to get energy and build muscle, skin, cartilage, and hair. The cells in the body need proteins called enzymes to speed up chemical reactions. Proteins also serve as hormones (chemical messengers) and antibodies.	cheese, eggs, lean meat, fish, and milk (some from cereal, grains, beans, rice, nuts)
Minerals calcium phosphorous magnesium potassium sodium	Minerals are needed for growth and maintenance of the body. They are also needed for digestive juices and fluids in and around cells. We get our minerals by eating plants or plant eating animals since the plants store the minerals they get from water or soil. You need tiny amounts of minerals such as copper, fluorine, iodine, iron, and zinc.	milk and milk products, cereals, meat, nuts, peas, whole-grain cereal, green-leafy vegetables
Vitamins A	needed for healthy skin and development of bones	liver, milk, green and yellow vegetables
B$_1$	necessary for changing starches and sugars from foods into energy (also called thiamine)	meat and whole grain cereals
B$_2$	used for chemical reactions during the body's use of food (also called riboflavin)	milk, cheese, fish, liver, green vegetables
B$_6$	used for chemical reactions in the body	various foods
Folate/ B$_{12}$	needed to form red blood cells and for a healthy nervous system	liver, green vegetables
Niacin	needed for cells to release energy into the body	liver, lean meats, fish, nuts
C	needed to maintain ligaments, tendons, and other supportive tissue	fruits & vegetables
D	helps the body use calcium for bones and teeth	fish, liver, sunlight
E	maintains cell membranes	vegetable oils, grain, cereal
Carbohydrates	used as fuel to power muscles, nerves, and build and repair body tissues; stored in liver for release when quick energy is needed	vegetable, fruits, bread and cereals

Nutrition and You *(cont.)*

Healthy You Puzzle

Puzzle Key: **A = nutrients**   **B = food source**   **C = used by body**

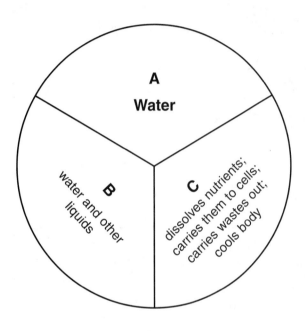

A
Water

B
water and other liquids

C
dissolves nutrients; carries them to cells; carries wastes out; cools body

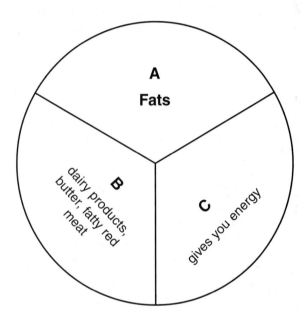

A
Fats

B
dairy products, butter, fatty red meat

C
gives you energy

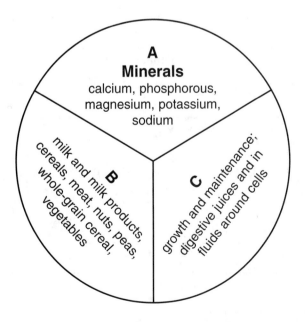

A
Minerals
calcium, phosphorous, magnesium, potassium, sodium

B
milk and milk products, cereals, meat, nuts, peas, whole-grain cereal, vegetables

C
growth and maintenance; digestive juices and in fluids around cells

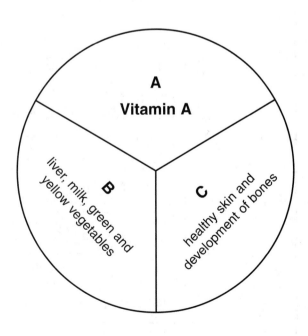

A
Vitamin A

B
liver, milk, green and yellow vegetables

C
healthy skin and development of bones

Healthy You Puzzle (cont.)

Puzzle Key: A = nutrients   B = food source   C = used by body

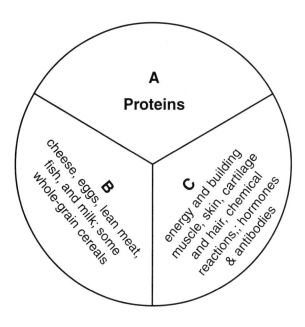

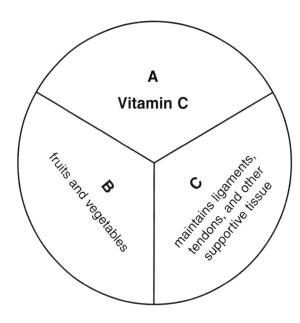

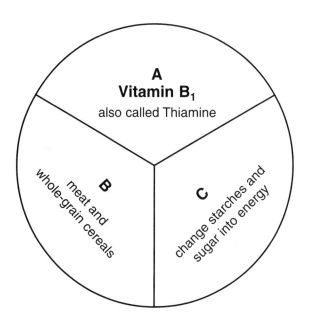

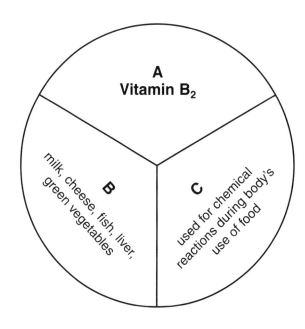

Healthy You Puzzle (cont.)

Puzzle Key: **A = nutrients**   **B = food source**   **C = used by body**

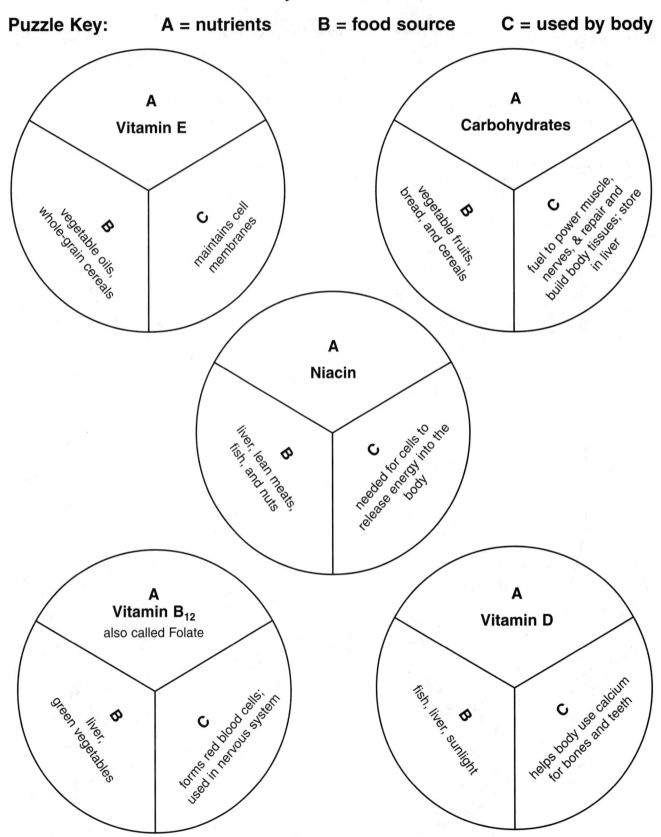

A
Vitamin E
B vegetable oils, whole-grain cereals
C maintains cell membranes

A
Carbohydrates
B vegetable fruits, bread, and cereals
C fuel to power muscle, nerves, & repair and build body tissues; store in liver

A
Niacin
B liver, lean meats, fish, and nuts
C needed for cells to release energy into the body

A
Vitamin B$_{12}$
also called Folate
B liver, green vegetables
C forms red blood cells; used in nervous system

A
Vitamin D
B fish, liver, sunlight
C helps body use calcium for bones and teeth

Eating for Good Health

To the Students: This guide will help you know what type of food you need each day and how many servings you should have to help your body stay healthy. This is a rough estimate of the foods you should eat to have a healthy diet. You will find you can never actually eat these recommended amounts every day. What really counts is that you try to eat the proportions of the different types of foods about equal to the circle graph shown below.

Use this guide and the chart on page 39 to help you complete the lunch menu on page 44.

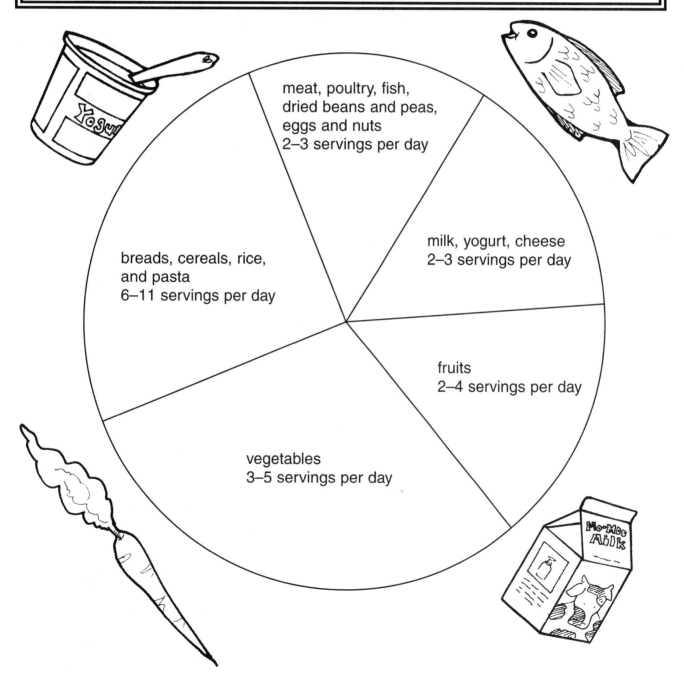

meat, poultry, fish, dried beans and peas, eggs and nuts
2–3 servings per day

milk, yogurt, cheese
2–3 servings per day

breads, cereals, rice, and pasta
6–11 servings per day

fruits
2–4 servings per day

vegetables
3–5 servings per day

Making Healthy Choices

Now it is your turn to decide what food should go into your body to keep it healthy. Review the Breakfast Menu from page 38 to see what percentage of the nutrients you have already eaten for one day. Use the guide on page 43 and the chart on page 39 to help you plan a healthy lunch to follow your breakfast. Read the nutrition facts on packaged foods you might eat for lunch to help you fill in the menu, remembering to increase the amounts if you eat more than the serving size shown on the package.

My Lunch Menu			
Nutrients	**Mass Daily Value**	**Mass Daily Value**	**Mass Daily Value**
	Food:_____ Serving Size:_____	Food:_____ Serving Size:_____	Food:_____ Serving Size:_____
Calories	_____	_____	_____
Calories from fat	_____	_____	_____
Fat	_____g _____%	_____g _____%	_____g _____%
Saturated Fat	_____g _____%	_____g _____%	_____g _____%
Cholesterol	_____mg _____%	_____mg _____%	_____mg _____%
Sodium	_____mg _____%	_____mg _____%	_____mg _____%
Potassium	_____mg _____%	_____mg _____%	_____mg _____%
Total Carbohydrate	_____g _____%	_____g _____%	_____g _____%
Dietary Fiber	_____g _____%	_____g _____%	_____g _____%
Sugars	_____g _____%	_____g _____%	_____g _____%
Protein	_____g _____%	_____g _____%	_____g _____%
Vitamin A	_____mg _____%	_____mg _____%	_____mg _____%
Vitamin C	_____mg _____%	_____mg _____%	_____mg _____%
Calcium	_____mg _____%	_____mg _____%	_____mg _____%
Iron	_____mg _____%	_____mg _____%	_____mg _____%
Vitamin D	_____mg _____%	_____mg _____%	_____mg _____%
Vitamin E	_____mg _____%	_____mg _____%	_____mg _____%
Thiamine	_____mg _____%	_____mg _____%	_____mg _____%
Riboflavin	_____mg _____%	_____mg _____%	_____mg _____%
Niacin	_____mg _____%	_____mg _____%	_____mg _____%
Vitamin B_6	_____mg _____%	_____mg _____%	_____mg _____%
Folate	_____mg _____%	_____mg _____%	_____mg _____%
Vitamin B_{12}	_____mg _____%	_____mg _____%	_____mg _____%
Phosphorus	_____mg _____%	_____mg _____%	_____mg _____%
Magnesium	_____mg _____%	_____mg _____%	_____mg _____%
Zinc	_____mg _____%	_____mg _____%	_____mg _____%
Copper	_____mg _____%	_____mg _____%	_____mg _____%

Nutrition and You *(cont.)*

How Healthy Is Your Diet?

Now that you have designed a breakfast and lunch menu for yourself, find your nutrition totals by completing the chart below. Do this by adding together the data recorded on the breakfast and lunch menus to see how much of each nutrient you have added to your body. The total nutrients should be less than shown in the "Daily Needs" column; remember that you have to eat dinner.

Summary Menu		
Nutrients	**Breakfast & Lunch**	**Daily Needs**
Calories	_____	2,200
Calories from fat	_____	600 or less
Fat	_____ g _____ %	65 g
Saturated Fat	_____ g _____ %	32 g or less
Cholesterol	_____ mg _____ %	300 mg or less
Sodium	_____ mg _____ %	2,400 mg or less
Potassium	_____ mg _____ %	
Total Carbohydrate	_____ g _____ %	
Dietary Fiber	_____ g _____ %	no less than 300 g for
Sugars	_____ g _____ %	both; keep sugars low
Protein	_____ g _____ %	45–60 g
Vitamin A	_____ mg _____ %	400* micrograms
Vitamin C	_____ mg _____ %	45 mg
Calcium	_____ mg _____ %	800–1,200 mg
Iron	_____ mg _____ %	10–12 mg
Vitamin D	_____ mg _____ %	10 micrograms
Vitamin E	_____ mg _____ %	
Thiamine B$_1$	_____ mg _____ %	1 mg
Riboflavin B$_2$	_____ mg _____ %	1 mg
Niacin	_____ mg _____ %	
Vitamin B$_6$	_____ mg _____ %	
Folate	_____ mg _____ %	
Vitamin B$_{12}$	_____ mg _____ %	
Phosphorus	_____ mg _____ %	*1 mg = 1,000 micrograms
Magnesium	_____ mg _____ %	
Zinc	_____ mg _____ %	
Copper	_____ mg _____ %	

On the back of this paper, write a brief summary to show how well you were able to design a healthy breakfast and lunch for yourself, and still leave room for eating more nutrients and calories for dinner. List any suggestions you have for improving your choices of food after doing these lessons.

This is My Body

Overview: *As a culmination of this unit, students will make a paper model of the body.*

Materials

- Body Parts (page 47)
- colored pens or crayons
- glue
- transparency of the human skeleton (page 19)
- pictures of muscles of the human body
- cardboard or tagboard

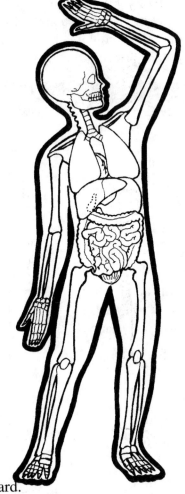

Activity

1. Now that they have completed their study of their bodies, tell the students they are going to make a paper copy of what they look like inside.

2. Distribute copies of page 47 to each child. Have them color the body parts as follows:

   - **brain**—gray
   - **esophagus**, **stomach**, and **duodenum**—yellow
   - **heart**—red
   - **lungs**—pink
   - **liver**—brown
   - **gall bladder**—green
   - **small intestine**—yellow
   - **large intestine**—pink

3. The students should cut out the body outline and glue it to cardboard.

4. Have students cut out the body parts and place them on the body outline. Let them check with other students to see if they agree with the placement and then glue these in place.

5. Show the students the skeleton transparency and let them sketch in the bones of the arms, hands, legs, and feet.

6. If available, show pictures of the muscles found in the human body and have students add some of those found in the arms and legs to one side of their body outline.

   (*Note:* See diagram above for the completed body picture.)

Closure

- If appropriate for these students, have them label their body parts.
- Cover the finished picture of the body with plastic wrap. Have the students take these home with the assignment of sharing them with family members and explaining some of what they learned from this study.

This is My Body *(cont.)*

Body Parts

Body Parts

Body Outline

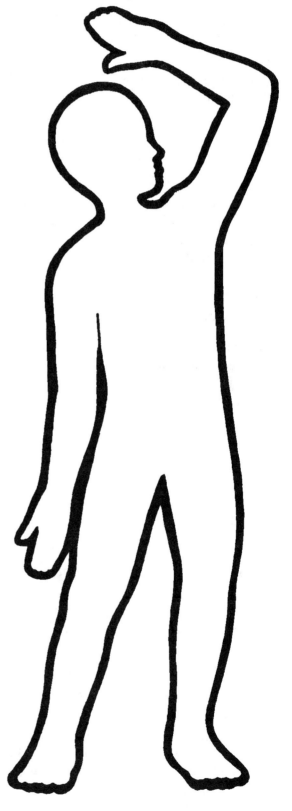

← brain

← heart

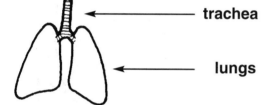

← trachea

← lungs

← liver

gall bladder

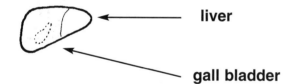

← duodenum

← stomach

esophagus

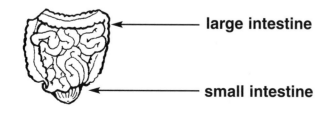

← large intestine

← small intestine

Teacher and Student Resources

Related Books

Allison, Linda. *Blood and Guts: A Working Guide to Your Own Insides.* Little, Brown, 1976. This book is full of great ideas to investigate the human body.

Bruun, Ruth Dowling and Bertel. *The Human Body: Your Body and How It Works.* Random House, 1982. Beautiful and accurate illustrations and easy-to-read text cover the topics of the regions of the body and the body systems.

Eyewitness Visual Dictionaries. *The Visual Dictionary of the Human Body.* Dorling Kindersley Books, 1991. This book contains vivid photographs and illustrations of human body parts.

Beckelman, Laurie. *The Human Body.* 1999 This book may be ordered from NSTA. (See below.) This large book (10" x 13"/25 cm x 33 cm) makes biology fascinating to kids in grades 3–6. It is organized as an incredible journey through the body's systems. Within each section are information about heroes of science, fun fact, and hands-on experiments.

Young, Ruth M. *Science/Literature Unit: Magic School Bus® Inside the Human Body.* Teacher Created Resources, Inc., 1996 This unit follows Ms. Frizzle and her students as they travel through the human body. Hands-on activities include learning about cells, nutrition, digestive, circulatory, nervous, skeletal and muscular systems.

Suppliers of Science Materials

Carolina Biological Resources (800) 334-5551 **http://www.carolina.com/**

Delta Education (800) 282-9560. Request a catalog of materials or order online at their Website.
http://www.delta-education.com/corp/info/ordernow.html
Supplies a wide variety of materials to support hands-on science in all areas from elementary to middle school.

Genesis, Inc. (800) 4PELLET. Request a catalog or order online at
http://www.pellet.com/
Supplies owl pellets as well as videos and teacher guides on this topic.

Insect Lore (800) LIVE BUG or
www.insectlore.com. Request a free catalog.
Provides an assortment of materials including Painted Lady butterfly and owl pellets.

National Science Resource Center **http://www.si.edu/nsrc/**
Resources for Teaching Elementary Science. National Science Resource Center, National Academy Press, Washington, DC., 1996. This is an outstanding resource guide to hands-on inquiry-centered elementary science curriculum materials and resources. Each reference in this guide has been carefully evaluated and is fully described, including addresses.
Read this book online or order it from: **http://www.nap.edu/catalog/4966.html**

National Science Teachers Association(NSTA)
http://www.nsta.org/ or the online catalog of materials at **http://store.nsta.org/**
This 53,000 member organization, founded in 1944, includes science teachers, science supervisors, administrators, scientists, and business and industry. Members receive a monthly professional journal, the bimonthly NSTA reports, discounts at the regional and national conventions and annual catalog of materials.